Why Don't Cars Run on Apple Juice?

Real Science Questions from Real Kids

Written by **Kira Vermond**   Illustrated by **Suharu Ogawa**

annick press

toronto • berkeley

Created in cooperation with the Ontario Science Centre

Designed by Paul Covello

Annick Press Ltd.

We acknowledge the support of the Canada Council for the Arts and the Ontario Arts Council, and the participation of the Government of Canada/la participation du gouvernement du Canada for our publishing activities.

Canada

ONTARIO ARTS COUNCIL
CONSEIL DES ARTS DE L'ONTARIO
an Ontario government agency
un organisme du gouvernement de l'Ontario

Library and Archives Canada Cataloguing in Publication
Title: Why don't cars run on apple juice? : real science questions from real kids / Kira Vermond ; Suharu Ogawa, illustrator.
Names: Vermond, Kira, author. | Ogawa, Suharu, 1979- illustrator.
Description: Includes index.
Identifiers: Canadiana (print) 20190066911 | Canadiana (ebook) 20190066938 | ISBN 9781773213026 (hardcover) | ISBN 9781773213057 (PDF) | ISBN 9781773213033 (EPUB) | ISBN 9781773213040 (Kindle)
Subjects: LCSH: Science—Miscellanea—Juvenile literature. | LCSH: Technology—Miscellanea—Juvenile literature.
Classification: LCC Q163 .V47 32019 | DDC j500—dc23

Published in the U.S.A. by Annick Press (U.S.) Ltd.
Distributed in Canada by University of Toronto Press.
Distributed in the U.S.A. by Publishers Group West.

Printed in China

annickpress.com
kiravermondkids.com
suharuogawa.com
ontariosciencecentre.ca

Also available as an e-book. Please visit annickpress.com/ebooks for more details.

For Nathan who asked why, Nadia who asked
how, and Dave who has all the answers.

—KV

For all the curious kids and kids-at-heart.

—SO

Contents

Introduction

Have you ever asked a question? Of course you have! Everything around us—from the deepest, darkest spot in the ocean to our twinkling stars above—fires up the imagination and inspires us to want to know more.

But there's a funny thing about questions: they always seem to lead to more questions. Check it out!

Question: "Is the center of the Earth hot?"

Answer: "Yes."

"How hot does it get?"

"If we can't travel to the center of the Earth to take its temperature, how do we measure it?"

"Is that why volcano lava is so hot?"

"What would happen if I threw a big diamond into a vat of lava?"

"If the human body is 18 percent carbon, can I be turned into a diamond?"

That's perfectly fine! The universe is a big, complex, and puzzling place, but humans have a powerful tool to help us make sense of it.

It's called SCIENCE.

Ask. Test. Repeat. It works.

Science isn't just a class at school. It's not a thing. Science is a process of asking questions in a way that helps us find answers that we can test to see if they're true. (At least based on what we know at the time.)

It's okay if the questions are hard and the answers confusing at first. (Scientists spend a lot of time scratching their heads.) That just means you need to keep asking more questions!

Real Kids, Real Questions

Every question came from kids who visited the Ontario Science Centre in Toronto, Canada—at a makerspace café called The Maker Bean, a place where café and technology meet. Here, their amazing and intriguing questions were laser-cut onto personalized wooden coasters, to use at the café to start science conversations with other visitors.

Educators and science researchers who work at the Centre came up with answers. But that's just the beginning! Hopefully this book will spark some new ideas and get you to ask yourself one very big question: What are you wondering about these days?

I've got questions about . . .

Whipping Up a Batch of Planet Earth

Pretend you live on a planet without air, water, or rock beneath your feet. What does that look like? (Hint: not much!)

Luckily, planet Earth is made up of amazing elements like oxygen, carbon, and sodium that give us everything we need to thrive. Check out these answers to some of your most elemental questions.

Why is ocean water salty?

Ever take a gulp of cool, refreshing . . . seawater? Blegh. Salty! It turns out there are loads of salt in our oceans. In fact, if you spread that salt across the Earth's entire land surface, it would form a layer 152 meters (500 feet) deep, roughly as tall as a 40-story building!

So how did it get there? It starts with rain. Water that falls from the sky is a tiny bit acidic. When that rainwater hits rocks on the ground, it dissolves the minerals in the rocks. Those minerals then enter rivers and streams and flow into the ocean. When the Sun comes out, the seawater heats up a little and evaporates, causing the remaining water to become even saltier.

Freshwater Fact!

Lakes and rivers contain salt and other minerals, too, but they are less salty than our oceans, so we can't taste it.

Why is some water turquoise and some water brown?

Water is actually perfectly clear. But a funny thing happens in large bodies of water such as rivers, lakes, or oceans. As sunlight passes through all the little droplets, the light splits up and scatters, creating a very faint blue tinge. Water reflects the blue sky above it, too.

Water also tends to pick up the color of what's in it.

Turquoise water found in mountain lakes and streams is often full of finely ground rock from ancient glaciers. The bright, bluish-green color we see is caused by the way light bounces off all those tiny rock particles.

Brown water might include a lot of stirred-up dirt, clay, or sand. One river in Alberta, Canada, sometimes looks pink! Iron and other colorful minerals flow through it.

If metal sinks, how do boats float?

Have you ever seen a towering cruise ship docked on dry land? It just doesn't seem possible that something that large, filled with people and made from metal, could stay afloat on water. Even a small fishing boat seems iffy. But boats rely on two nifty science tricks called displacement and up-thrust to keep from sinking.

If a boat weighs less than the amount of water it pushes aside (displaces), it floats. All that displaced water needs to go somewhere, so it thrusts up to the water's surface. This balancing act—the boat sinking down and the water rushing up—keeps the boat afloat.

And don't forget: unlike a dense bar of metal, which would most certainly sink, a boat's interior is full of air, making the boat lighter than the water below it. That helps, too.

How does gravity keep us down?

Go ahead. Set this book down for a moment.

What just happened? Did it float away? Unless you're reading this in space, your book probably didn't go anywhere. Thank gravity.

Gravity is an invisible force that pulls objects toward each other (in this case, the book toward the Earth). Without gravity, we couldn't survive on this planet. It keeps our atmosphere in place and our air close to us so we can breathe. And while Earth's gravity keeps you from flying into space, that's nothing compared to the Sun's gravitational pull. It's so strong that entire planets spin in orbit around the Sun! Without that gravity, Earth would float away from the Sun and become too cold to live on.

No one knows exactly how gravity works, but Albert Einstein had a theory that goes a long way toward explaining the mysterious force. He believed the entire universe is filled with the fabric of space and time.

Imagine dropping a really heavy bowling ball in the middle of a trampoline. What happens? The ball creates a deep well in the center, right? Now imagine placing a marble at the edge of the trampoline. It would roll toward the bowling ball, unless you and your friends started bouncing!

Earth is just like the bowling ball. When dropped deep into the fabric of space, it creates a "gravity well." And, like the marble, you can't jump out of it. You just get sucked back to Earth.

Only something moving really fast can get out of the well and escape Earth's gravity. Rockets can do it—by traveling at speeds faster than 40,000 kilometers (24,855 miles) an hour!

Where does wind come from?

Wind. We use it to fly kites, dry our clothes, sail our boats, and even power our houses. On winter days, it can also chill us to our bones. Brrr! Wind is so much a part of our lives, we don't often wonder why air moves around in the first place. To answer that question, it helps to understand two important rules about air:

1. Hot air rises and cool air sinks.

2. Air pressure is the weight of air molecules pushing down on the Earth. The higher you go, the less air pressure there is.

Got it? Good.

As the Sun heats up areas of land, the air gets hotter, rises, and leaves behind an area where there's less air pressure. Cooler, heavier air that hangs out over oceans and large lakes swoops in and takes its place. The quick movement of those air molecules is what we call wind.

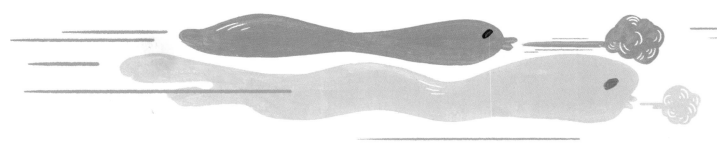

Why can't we feel the Earth moving?

Here's a wild thought. As you sit and read this book, you're also moving at an incredible 460 meters (1,500 feet) per second as Earth spins on its axis and rotates around the Sun. So why don't you feel it?

Unlike riding a bicycle, with the air whipping through your hair, the scenery whizzing by, and the bumpy road below your wheels, you don't experience Earth's movement as a sensation.

Although our scenery changes—the Sun, stars, and Moon seem to travel (slowly) across our sky—there is no rough road underneath Earth to give us the sense that we're going anywhere. What's more, everything around us is moving at exactly the same speed as everything else. Oceans, cities, trees, giraffes, your grumpy school principal. You name it.

It's kind of like flying in a large airplane. Even though you're traveling 805 kilometers (500 miles) per hour, unless you look out the window, you might not feel like you're moving at all.

What came first, the tree or the seed?

The tree. Kind of. In fact, all plants and trees on Earth can be traced back to a teeny tiny green cell that captured chlorophyll (a chemical that absorbs sunlight and turns it into energy). This happened about 1.6 billion years ago. Eventually those green-colored, sludgy bacteria evolved into more complex plants.

Now fast-forward more than a billion years.

Fossil records show that tree-like plants developed during the Devonian period, 416 million to 358 million years ago—about 140 million years before the dinosaurs showed up! The first trees used spores to reproduce (like ferns and mosses do today). These specimens could live only in moist areas and swamps. It was only when some trees eventually developed seeds that could be carried around by the wind that baby trees started to grow in drier areas, too.

Put the "See" in Seed!

How can you tell if you're looking at a spore or a seed? Spores are microscopic organisms that contain only a single cell and are invisible to the human eye. Seeds are larger and more complex, so if you can see it, it's a seed.

How do trees know about seasons?

They don't. At least not the way you think about winter, spring, summer, and autumn. Instead, trees gather signals from their environment—daily sunshine, nighttime temperature, and rainfall—and that information triggers them to drop leaves in the fall or push sap up to the tallest branches in early spring.

Here's how it would work for a leafy deciduous tree in Canada:

Nights are getting longer in September. Temperatures are dropping, too.

The tree takes these two pieces of information and decides, "Whoa! Time to stop making food and get ready for some stressful times."

Goodbye, leaves.

But what about a tree growing in a tropical country where it's always warm and daylight hours are steady year round? Take a look:

Here comes the drought season. Things are getting a little parched. Time to lose those thirsty leaves and save valuable energy.

THUNDER! LIGHTNING!

The rainy season triggers the tree to sprout leaves again so it can grow tall and strong. No calendar required.

Is there enough food in the world?

Yes. There are nearly 8 billion people alive today (and that number is growing), and there is enough food to feed every single adult and child. Still, about a billion people go to sleep hungry each night. How can that be?

Sadly, some families don't have enough land to grow the food they need or the money to buy it. It also can be difficult to farm or transport food in a war-torn country, especially if corrupt politicians won't help their starving people. Meanwhile in wealthier nations, a lot of groceries get thrown out. In 2018, Americans tossed 13.6 million kilograms (150,000 tons) of food each day—equal to about half a kilogram (1 pound) per person.

Don't Chuck That Cheese!

Cutting food waste at home might not seem like it would help hungry families in faraway countries. It's not like you can seal up your leftover mashed potatoes and pop them in the mail. But remember: growing, producing, and transporting food requires a lot of energy. And all of that energy results in greenhouse gases being pumped into the Earth's atmosphere.

If everyone buys only the food they need, our planet will remain healthier longer—with enough nourishing agricultural land to make sure all people get enough to eat!

Why don't cars run on apple juice?

Technically they can, although we'd have to make many changes to our cars' engines first. Some people have already converted their diesel cars to run on cooking oil and even garbage! Why not apple juice, too?

Today, most vehicles use gasoline, made from crude oil pumped out of the ground in the form of black, slippery petroleum. Each liter of gas (about a quarter of a gallon) contains 8,000 calories. A calorie measures energy, and 8,000 of them would give the average 10-year-old enough energy for four days—if gas were food, that is. But apple juice? A liter contains 466 calories, not even half a day's worth of energy.

Because apple juice contains less zippy power, cars would need bigger fuel tanks, or they'd have to fill up way more often. That's too bad. Imagine how amazing gas stations might smell if vehicles used apple juice as fuel. Warm apple pie!

CHAPTER 2

I've got questions about . . .

Creeping, Crawling Living Things

Sure, there are nearly 8 billion humans on Earth today, but that's nothing compared to the whopping 8.7 million *species* of creatures slithering, swimming, sprinting, and scurrying over the planet. (Yep, including 22.8 billion chickens!) Here are some wild facts about a few of them.

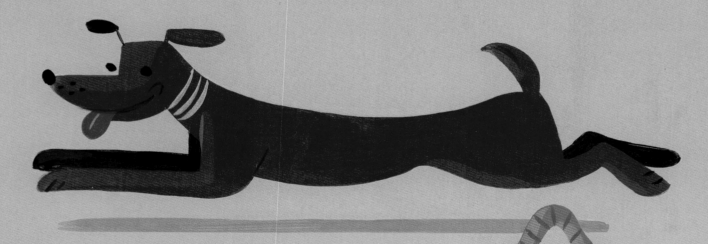

Why do worms come out when it rains?

When earthworms feel the vibration created by a downpour, it's as though their little worm brains think, "Great! The highway just opened. It's so much more convenient than this dirt road." Rain allows earthworms to quickly travel from one place to another. Slinking above ground is a lot easier than tunneling through soil, which requires plenty of energy and time.

Worms don't travel above ground when it's sunny, though, because their damp bodies would dry out too quickly.

Breathe Easy

Earthworms don't have lungs. They breathe through their skin. Damp, moist, and slimy skin is best for absorbing oxygen into the bloodstream.

Why don't jellyfish have brains?

Brains are amazing, but they use a lot of energy. That's okay for humans and other mammals because we have very complex body systems. It helps to have a hardworking brain that can send, receive, and organize all the information that comes in from our nerves when we touch, taste, hear, smell, or see the world around us.

But compared to humans, jellyfish have much simpler body systems. They can get by without a central brain. Instead, they have a neural network—lots of interconnected nerves. Without a brain sucking up energy, jellyfish don't need to eat as much and can spend their time swimming or darting away from predators.

Can rats burp?

Nope. They can't vomit either. (Although rats are ticklish. Go figure!) Below the esophagus, rats have a very tight sphincter. That's a valve that allows air, water, and food to travel only one way: down into the stomach.

Not being able to vomit can actually be pretty dangerous. If a rat eats something poisonous, there's no way to get it out of the body quickly. Luckily, rats are supersmart! They use their sense of taste and smell to decide if something is safe to munch on. Or they'll eat a minuscule amount . . . and wait to see if they start to feel sick. If the toxic food or poison doesn't pass the safety test, the rat will communicate with other rats to avoid it.

One more thing: if a rat can't burp, you might be wondering what happens to all that trapped air in its belly. Easy. It farts.

Why do we have different faces but ants do not?

Who says they don't? With at least 12,000 different ant species in the world, there are bound to be differences between them. In fact, using magnification, experts can tell ant species apart simply by looking at their facial features. Some have smaller heads or larger mandibles, or their antennae are positioned farther back. Most of us won't notice these small variations, though. To an untrained eye, all ant faces look pretty much the same.

Even so, you can see many differences between ant species just by looking at them. Ants come in many colors and sizes. Some have wings and others don't. Others devour everything in their path. Stand back!

BAM!

The trap-jaw ant has powerful mandibles that it slams on the ground to propel itself backward and away from predators!

How do whales sleep?

You mean, why don't they drown when they catch some zzzz's underwater? After all, whales are mammals, not fish, and they need to come up for air using their blowholes to breathe.

Luckily, whales' bodies have adapted to their watery environment in a few different ways. Some swim to the water's surface and fall asleep while floating. Many whales slumber for only a few minutes at a time. Others sleep using only . . . half a brain! One side of the brain slumbers and the other side stays awake enough to help the animal swim and head up to the surface to breathe.

Two-for-One Special

Humpback whales have two blowholes to breathe through, just like you have two nostrils!

It's a Scientific Fact!

Sperm whales sometimes gather together in groups and sleep vertically, with their tails down and blowholes up close to the ocean's surface.

Why can't you live with a wolf?

Quick answer: wolves are dangerous!

But why do we think wolves are scary when they look so much like dogs, our devoted companions? Probably because wolves just haven't hung out with us long enough.

Dogs used to be a lot like wolves, but for tens of thousands of years, they have been part of our human family and have evolved alongside people. Slowly, many of their former wolf-like instincts disappeared.

Just consider a study that compared how dogs and wolves solve problems. Both were put in a locked room with scrumptious treats hidden behind the door. The wolves either grew exhausted trying to open the door to get at their meal or eventually gave up. Meanwhile, dogs tried hard, but if there was a human nearby, the pooches stopped and looked to the person for aid. It was as if they were saying, "Hey, you know how to do this. Help me out here, would you?"

Dogs' behavior has altered so they now rely on and trust people. But wolves? Not so much.

If a dog says "woof!" will other dogs understand?

Dogs don't communicate the way people do. In other words, it's not as simple as "Woof! Woof! Woof!" meaning, "Hey, buddy, how are you doing?" Instead, dogs use their whole bodies to connect with other canines. They wag their tails to show they're happy or unthreatening, pant when they're nervous, and open their eyes WIDE as a warning to other dogs to back off!

So yes, woofs, barks, and growls all mean something to other dogs, but think of them as single words. When dogs want to communicate a whole "sentence," they'll combine those sounds with plenty of other body language.

Go Wild (at Twilight)

Ever wonder why your dog wakes up at the crack of dawn, sleeps all day, and then can't wait to play after dinner? It turns out dogs and wolves are considered "crepuscular." They're most active at dawn and dusk.

What's the smartest animal on Earth?

That all depends on what you mean by smart. There are different kinds of intelligence. For instance . . .

• **Crows** can solve some puzzles kids can't even figure out! In one study, they dropped pebbles into a small-mouthed container to raise the water level to get at a floating toy. The children in the study never made that mental leap.

• **Dolphins** can recognize themselves in a mirror. Most other animals don't pass this test. They think they're seeing another animal and run away or try to fight it!

• **Schools of fish** show "swarm intelligence." They move together in perfect formation without banging into each other.

If your definition of smart includes being able to solve long mathematical problems, then humans are the most intelligent animals on the planet. But even amongst humans, our "smarts" depend on our environment and experiences. A person living in the Amazon jungle may be better at identifying tropical plants than a professor in Alaska, for instance.

How many unfound species are there in the world?

Millions! Studies have predicted that Earth is home to 8.7 million species—but we've only logged 1.8 million of them so far. Why so few? Some species like bacteria, fungi, and lichen are not easy to identify. In other cases, extreme habitats, like gas-filled caves, airless mountains, and bone-dry deserts, are difficult for scientists to explore in order to find new insects, plants, and animals. The ocean probably holds the most mysteries.

Sadly, scientists estimate that 150 to 200 species of plants, insects, and animals become extinct every day. That's a thousand times faster than anything the world has seen since the dinosaurs were wiped out around 66 million years ago.

Many species will disappear before we ever get to meet them.

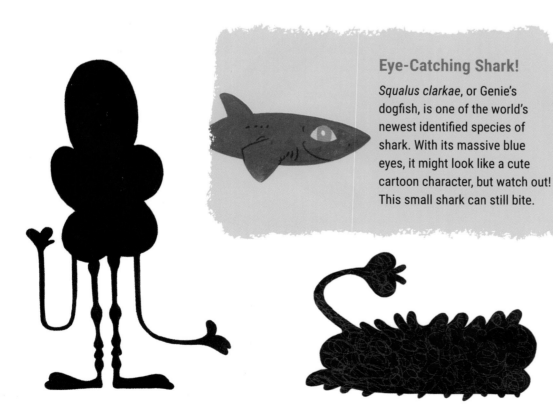

Eye-Catching Shark!

Squalus clarkae, or Genie's dogfish, is one of the world's newest identified species of shark. With its massive blue eyes, it might look like a cute cartoon character, but watch out! This small shark can still bite.

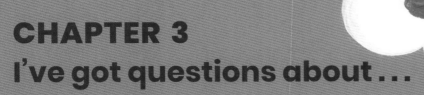

CHAPTER 3
I've got questions about . . .

Human Bodies from the Inside Out

Did you know blood makes up about 8 percent of your body weight?
The skin you're in houses your brain, heart, and a whole lot more.
But how do all those body bits and pieces work? Here's the scoop
on your amazing—and sometimes gross—anatomy.

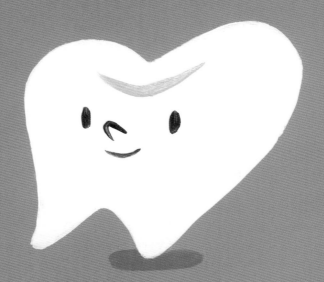

Why do my toots smell?

Whew! Crack a window! Toots (also called flatulence) smell because many of the foods we eat can't be completely broken down by our bodies, especially those that come from plants like fruits, vegetables, beans, and nuts. All of the leftover material ends up in the large intestine, where it becomes a tasty treat for bacteria—tiny creatures that live there. The leftovers from the bacteria's feast—the waste—is our poop. But bacteria create their own waste, too. Sometimes, it's stinky gas.

Flatulence does have one thing going for it. Because it's often caused by eating fresh and healthy plant-based foods, blowing stinky gas from time to time isn't necessarily a bad thing!

Silent . . . but Deadly

The longer food stays in the intestine, the more it ferments (like when milk goes sour) and the smellier those toots get.

Why do you always have to go to the bathroom?

What a pain. You're in the middle of a test at school and—oh no! You've got to go. Again!

Some people think that pee and poop (which are also known as urine and feces) are embarrassing and annoying (or, let's face it, super-hilarious!). But going to the bathroom is a good thing. Eating, drinking, and producing waste from material your body doesn't need is a sign that you're alive and healthy.

In fact, if you have a nourishing diet and drink enough fluid, you'll probably need to hit the restroom at least four to six times a day. If you're dehydrated and thirsty, you'll go a little less.

Why is poo brown?

Unicorns might poop rainbows, but alas, human poo is just dull brown. While the food we eat is often quite colorful—think orange carrots, red strawberries, and green salads—once it hits our digestive system, it gets churned up and goes through chemical changes. Check out what happens to this orange slice.

Whee! After being swallowed, it enters the esophagus.

Down into the stomach . . .

Through the intestines . . .

And waves hello to the liver.

The liver sends brownish-green bile and recycled red blood cells into the food, where they all get mixed up with bacteria that live in the gut. Those bacteria start a chemical reaction that turns poo brown.

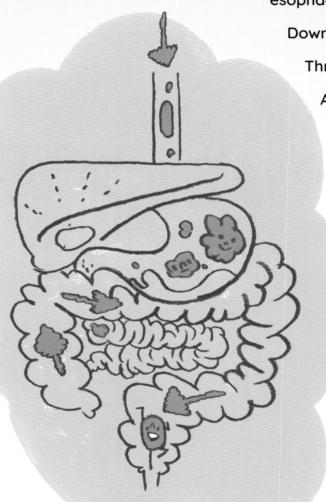

A Pooper-Duper Fact!

Newborn babies' poop isn't brown. It's green—though the color is so dark it can look black. That's because most of the time, there's no bacteria in it yet—only bile and other fluids.

Why are we tired when we run?

It takes a lot of energy for us to move our muscles to run. And muscles in motion also need more oxygen, which is why you breathe faster and harder once you pick up speed. When we use up too much of our energy, we need to build it up again. That feeling of being tired is a surefire sign it's time to stop and rest. Getting enough sleep and eating healthy food help our bodies renew our energy so we can get back out there and play!

Why can't humans breathe underwater?

Because our lungs aren't powerful enough! People breathe air—made up of mostly nitrogen and oxygen—through their noses and mouths. That air enters the lungs, which are filled with branches and air sacks called alveoli. These are surrounded by tiny blood vessels. This blood picks up the air's oxygen before it moves on to the rest of your body.

Fish are a bit different, even though the concept is similar. Fish have gills that can extract oxygen from water.

Here's the thing about air versus water, though. Air has about 20 times more oxygen in it than the same volume of water. It's also much lighter than water, so it takes a lot less work to move it. In order to breathe water, your lungs would have to be HUGE!

Fish get away with breathing underwater because they're cold-blooded. That means they don't need as much energy-giving oxygen to live.

But you still wouldn't be able to take a big, fresh breath of water, even if your lungs were gigantic. That's because human lungs can't extract the oxygen from H_2O.

Why do humans have two eyes?

Scientists can't really say for sure why humans evolved this way, but here's what we do know: two eyes are better than one. Each eye sees something slightly different and sends those images to the brain. They're then stitched together to create a 3D image. The result? Depth perception!

Depth perception allows us to determine the distance between things. It's a trait that would have come in handy back in prehistoric days. If a hungry lion was chasing us, it obviously helped to know how close it was as we ran for our lives!

But why two eyes and not three, eight, or seventeen? Wouldn't more eyes be better? Probably not. If more eyes gave us an advantage, humans would have evolved with them over time. Maybe too many images would confuse our brains. Or multiple eyes would use too much energy, or even make our heads way too big for our necks to hold!

Why do teeth fall out?

Unlike fish and reptiles, which seem to lose and grow teeth any old time (hello, shark-tooth necklaces!), humans typically grow only two sets of teeth during their lives: a primary set (a.k.a. baby teeth) and a permanent, adult set. Each tooth has a special job: some are meant for ripping, others for chewing.

Babies have small jaws, so they have space for only 20 tiny teeth. As kids' mouths grow, the roots of this starter set dissolve inside the gums. Those primary teeth fall out to make way for 32 bigger, better chompers.

These permanent teeth—if taken care of—are meant to last. It would require too much energy to grow new ones!

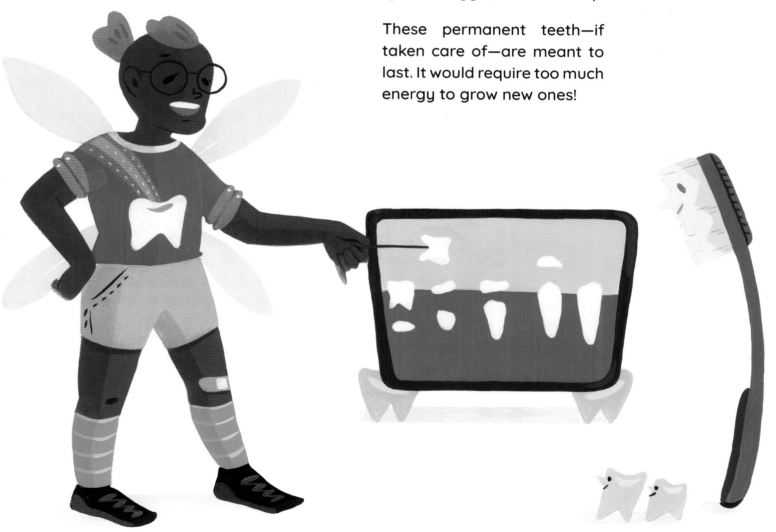

Why is everybody different?

All of us are unique, from our hair all the way to our tickly toes. How we get that way comes down to our deoxyribonucleic acid, also known as DNA.

DNA is a really long, coiled-up molecule found in your cells. It contains the instructions for everything your body needs to do—like growing fingernails or digesting a big bowl of ice cream. This epic to-do list is written in a special code that uses only four "letters" called nucleotides. It takes 3 billion of those letters to write out all the instructions!

The code is about 99.9 percent the same in each person. But some of the nucleotides are arranged differently in all of us. One combination might give you black hair instead of red, or brown eyes instead of green. Other combinations will give you a squeaky voice instead of a low one, or the ability to bend your thumbs . . . all . . . the . . . way . . . back. Families inherit similar DNA structures, but they're not exactly the same. That's why you might look a little like Great-Uncle Herman, but there's still plenty about you that's different.

Stretch It Out

If you unraveled all the DNA strands in your body and stretched them out, they would circle the solar system . . . twice!

How do people think without language?

You do it all the time. Let's say you're drawing a picture of a house. Chances are you're not saying to yourself, "House! Window! Door!" as you scratch pencil against paper.

You visualize the house. You think in images.

Even babies think before they understand words. Rather than thinking, "If I cry really hard, Dad's going to come pick me up!" they just wail because they know from experience that it works. But some people maintain that's not real thinking, that only proper thoughts use language.

Not so fast. Many of Albert Einstein's most amazing intellectual breakthroughs happened with numbers instead of language.

Using words to think works in many situations, like when you're sending a text or giving a presentation in class. But our brains often adjust the way we think to fit the task we're doing.

Why do people find things funny? Why is everyone so funny?

How do oceans say hello? They wave!

Even if you didn't find that joke hilarious, chances are something in your brain went, "Ping! That's supposed to be funny." Humor is part of what makes us human. It's also highly personal. What's funny to a person in England might not be as funny to someone in Japan.

Experts who study humor have many theories about why we tend to laugh at some things and not others, no matter where we live. For instance, people sometimes laugh at situations they don't expect. The surprise creates a strong emotion and laughing relieves the tension. Tension relief is a big part of humor and has been shown to decrease anxiety, fear, and even physical pain.

That ocean joke? If you chuckled, you were probably experiencing the little thrill of "getting" the joke.

Then there's the "superiority theory." It states that people enjoy laughing at the misfortunes of others. We feel happy knowing we're better off than someone else. The Germans even have a word for this: *schadenfreude*.

Funny word, huh?

Why do people need to sleep?

Short answer? We don't know. But scientists have a few theories.

Here's one. People and animals need sleep to repair their bodies and restore what was lost during the day. That means growing muscle and healing tissue. Sleep also helps us conserve energy so we have enough when we really need it, like during gym class.

It's also thought that healthy sleep helps us retain information. As you go through your day, your brain picks up a ton of information that's stored as short-term memory. Sleep takes all that data, processes it overnight, and moves it into our long-term memory bank to be accessed later. This is one of the reasons that, without sleep, you might forget to grab your lunch (and homework) for school!

Have a Test? Sleep on It

Researchers have discovered that people remember facts better if they learn them right before going to bed. Want to ace your next test? Don't wait until the morning to study. Review your work before falling asleep—and then let your amazing brain do the rest.

Why do we die?

Our bodies are amazing. Our many systems work together and give us everything we need to live. We have a respiratory system that helps us breathe, a digestive system that gives us energy from food, and a circulatory system that moves blood through our veins so every part of us gets oxygen and nutrients.

When one of those systems no longer works, we die. There might be an accident that injures the heart muscle so blood can't circulate anymore. Or perhaps an illness damages the lungs and makes breathing impossible. Sometimes people live so long, their systems stop working as well as they used to, like car parts that get rusty or break after working for years.

If one system fails, other systems struggle until the body shuts down and dies.

CHAPTER 4

I've got questions about . . .

Stars, Moons, Planets, and Outer Space

Look up! See those thousands of stars visible to the human eye?
Space is hardly a big void of inky nothingness. Scientists are unearthing
all kinds of incredible discoveries about the night sky.

The next few questions are really *out there*.

Are there creatures on other planets?

At this moment, Earth is the only place we know of where life exists. And no wonder. We have everything we need. Our planet is neither too hot nor too cold. We also have liquid water, which is important for supporting life.

As we learn more about the other planets and even moons in our solar system, we are discovering that there might be other places where life could exist. Perhaps ice-covered planets are actually hiding liquid-water oceans below the surface, and perhaps tiny things do live there.

On Earth, we call the type of species that could exist in these conditions extremophiles—microscopic organisms that thrive in really strange places such as the frigid Arctic permafrost or boiling hydrothermal vents on the ocean floor. If creatures can live in these extreme conditions on Earth, what's to stop them from living in similar places on other planets?

Besides, our Milky Way galaxy contains *at least* 100 billion planets. With a number like that, many scientists believe there must be at least a few other planets that are home to other creatures.

How do the stars stay in the sky?

Let's say you threw a ball as high as you could. Even if you were the best baseball pitcher around, that ball would still eventually fall back to Earth. Gravity pulls it down. But what if you could throw that ball so hard it actually escaped Earth's strong gravitational pull? It would stay up in orbit around our planet. (And probably earn you a world record for strongest arm.)

Stars are so far away from the Earth that our gravity doesn't pull them down toward us, either.

Up, Up, and Away . . .

Due to the Moon's weak gravity, a person who weighs 45 kilograms (100 pounds) on Earth would weigh only 7.7 kilograms (17 pounds) on the Moon.

What happens inside a black hole?

No one really knows what's inside a black hole, but here's a cool new word for you: spaghettification. That's right. Think long, stringy spaghetti. That's what might happen to you if you entered a black hole— an area in space where gravity pulls so hard even light can't escape. The theory goes that if you were traveling feet-first into a black hole, the gravitational pull would be stronger at your feet than your head, so your entire body would S - - - - T - - - - R - - - - E - - - T - - - - C - - - H !

At least, that's what some astronomers and scientists believe. No one knows for sure what would happen to someone inside a black hole. (It's not exactly an experiment you can try at home, right?) Experts do understand enough about gravity to make some very educated guesses, though.

Leaving Clues Behind

Black holes are so dark we can't see them, but we know they're there because scientists can view how their intense gravity affects objects around them. Wheee!

Will another asteroid hit Earth?

Yes, definitely. But try not to worry. Our planet gets dinged by space rocks all the time, although they're usually quite tiny and do little damage. Luckily, Earth is small and has very little gravity, at least when you compare it to other massive planets like Jupiter, so we have less chance of drawing asteroids toward us and being hit. No need to stress about having asteroid drills at school!

A Celestial Kaboom!!!

About once a year, a car-sized asteroid zips into Earth's atmosphere and burns up in the sky before hitting the ground. Meanwhile, Earth gets hit with tons of dust and sand-sized particles every day.

Why are planets round?

Ever try blowing a soap bubble using a wand that has a triangle or square shape on the end of it? You never get triangle- or square-shaped bubbles—they always become round. That's because all the tiny particles in the soap bubble "skin" are attracted to each other, which pulls the bubble into a sphere. No points. No sharp edges.

In space, a similar thing happens to very big objects like stars, planets, and moons. Like the skin on the soap bubble, the attractive force of their own gravity pulls these objects into spheres. Even so, many planets aren't perfectly round. Take the Earth. Because it rotates on its axis, there are forces that pull it outward—so our planet's sphere is actually a little bit squished.

If I were to sneeze in outer space, would my head blow up?

Thankfully nobody's head has ever exploded from getting the sniffles in space. In fact, not much happens at all. According to astro-snots (oops, sorry, that would be astronauts) who have sneezed in microgravity, the force gently propelled them in the direction opposite to where their noses were pointing. Kind of like a thruster on a backpack. In other words, the laws of physics still apply. For every action, there is an equal and opposite reaction.

Can sound move in space?

No, it can't—or, at least, if there's sound out there, humans can't hear it. Sound needs stuff—think the air in your room, the water in a swimming pool, or your desk at school—to travel through and create sound waves. These waves bounce back and forth quickly, like a slinky toy. The denser the stuff (think a metal door versus a screen one), the faster those waves travel.

On Earth, sound moves through air, water, or even solids like metal. But in space, any molecules—interstellar gases or old stardust—are so spread out that the sound waves they might carry would be too slow and low for the human ear to hear.

What causes a solar eclipse?

One word: coincidences!

- Earth orbits around the Sun.

- Our Moon orbits around Earth.

- The Sun is 400 times bigger than the Moon.

- But, by total coincidence . . .

- Our Moon is approximately 400 times closer to planet Earth than the Sun!

From time to time the Moon moves between the Sun and Earth. The distance is perfect for it to block out the light of the Sun and cast a shadow on an area of Earth.

What are the odds of all these factors lining up perfectly? A total eclipse (one where the Moon completely covers the Sun's light) happens only about every year and a half, although it's only visible from a few places on Earth each time.

"It's Like Being on Another Planet!"

That's how some people describe what it's like to experience a total eclipse of the Sun. During those minutes of darkness, shadows change, flowers shut tight, and bats start swooping in the murky daytime sky.

Why do diamonds rain onto Saturn?

Well, we're not 100 percent sure they do, but that's a theory scientists are testing in labs on Earth today. Here's the thinking: Diamonds are formed when carbon (the element you find in your graphite pencil tip) is exposed to extreme heat and pressure. It turns out there's a lot of carbon in the atmosphere around our outer planets—Uranus and Neptune—and some around Saturn and Jupiter, too. That's because one of the main gases in their atmospheres is methane (yep, just like the stuff you find in cow farts), which is made up of carbon and hydrogen.

We also know that these outer planets are hit with ferocious lightning storms! The combination of sizzling hot lightning and methane creates carbon soot. As these tiny particles of carbon fall toward a planet's core, they're exposed to crushing pressure and heat. With enough of it, those diamonds could even liquefy. Voilà! Diamond rain.

If the universe is expanding, then what's outside the universe?

Ready to break your brain? Good. Here's a popular answer for you: nothing and everything. In other words, the universe isn't expanding into anything. It's just expanding. Everything that could possibly exist anytime and anywhere is part of the cosmos. There's no beginning, no middle, and no end.

See that thing outside our universe? It's part of our universe! How about that black bit of nothing all around the universe? Still universe. Hey, you forgot the area beyond that. Sorry. It's part of the universe, too. (We could play this game for hours . . .)

Imagine the universe is an expanding balloon and you're a tiny ant that lives on its two-dimensional surface. If you were to crawl in a straight line in any direction, you'd eventually end up in the same spot again. And every time you make the journey, it takes longer as the balloon gets bigger and bigger.

Needless to say, our human brains have a tough time with this concept because we're so used to things that start and end, or have shapes we can see. Maybe that's the reason some people really like a newfangled theory that suggests our universe is just one little bubble floating around with many universes in a vast "multiverse."

But of course that just raises the question: What's outside our multiverse?

See? Mind blown. Go on and flip the page. You'll find more big questions there.

CHAPTER 5

I've got questions about . . .

Big Ideas Past, Present, and Future

CAUTION! There are some BIG questions that are so hard to define, they deserve their own chapter. Check out these mind-blowing, keep-you-up-at-night scientific theories that might just change how you experience EVERYTHING around you. (Don't say you haven't been warned.)

How did we discover the Big Bang?

Look up at the night sky. Serene and peaceful, right? Wrong! At this very minute, all the galaxies are zipping away from each other. Our entire universe is expanding! That's what Edwin Hubble (1889–1953) discovered back in 1929 while looking at galaxies through a strong telescope and making calculations.

That discovery led to a big question: If everything is flying apart now, what would we find if we looked at time in reverse and watched the universe shrink?

The obvious answer would be that at some point—think 13.7 billion years ago—everything in the universe was tightly packed together. But there also had to be an event that made it all fly out and start expanding. We call this event the Big Bang.

Big Bang Blunder

When you hear the words "Big Bang," you probably imagine a GIANT EXPLOSION. Try again. Think of the Big Bang as an expansion of space, matter, and even time that started in an instant. Like a cake suddenly rising in the oven or blowing up a balloon that just gets bigger . . . and bigger . . . and bigger.

An Amazing Big Bang Accident!

Between 1964 and 1965, two radio astronomers named Arno Penzias and Robert Wilson made an incredible discovery completely by accident. While attempting to use a strong antenna for their own space experiment, they kept hearing a weird noise that sounded like fuzzy static coming from every direction. It was ruining their research. The buzz had to go! The two men tried everything to figure out the source of the noise.

Was it radiation noise from the Milky Way? Nope.

It didn't come from aliens.

It wasn't radio interference from nearby New York City.

Pigeons nesting in the antenna? They removed the birds, but the odd buzzing remained.

Finally, the two radio astronomers heard about a physicist named Robert Dicke who had a theory: if the Big Bang really had happened, there would be an ancient, cosmic radiation filling the universe. It could cause the sound Penzias and Wilson heard.

Eureka! Penzias's and Wilson's discovery of cosmic microwave background (CMB) radiation earned them a Nobel Prize in Physics.

Why are dinosaurs so BIG?

We actually don't know why some dinosaurs grew to be as big and heavy as a hundred crocodiles. Maybe large dinos were simply harder to kill and eat. Dinosaurs with long necks could also reach the tallest, most succulent leaves. Did they evolve over millions of years to grow in a way that would keep them safer and well fed? At this point, scientists still aren't sure.

It's a little easier to answer how some dinosaurs were able to survive at their massive size. For starters, their bones were quite light and hollow, much like birds' bones are today. (This is one of the reasons scientists now say that today's birds are actually the last remaining dinosaurs!) And like birds, their bodies contained air sacks to allow air to flow through their lungs. Being both light and strong made it easier for these dinosaurs to get around despite their gargantuan size.

Patagotitan mayorum: The BIGGEST Dino of All?

In 2013 a man in Argentina discovered a half-buried dinosaur bone at the farm where he worked. It was hard to miss. Once uncovered, the thighbone was 2.4 meters (8 feet) long! It belonged to a long-necked dinosaur, which paleontologists called the *Patagotitan mayorum*. They now believe this sauropod is the biggest dinosaur that ever lived. Today you can see a cast of the gargantuan dinosaur at the American Museum of Natural History in New York City.

Big Picture

Lived

102 million years ago

Weight

54,000–72,500 kilograms (60–80 tons)

Length

40 meters (130 feet)

That's the same as:

- 14 elephants
- a Boeing 737-900
- a seven-story building
- two tractor-trailer trucks end to end

How do we really know a meteor killed the dinosaurs?

It didn't. That would be an asteroid, which is much larger!

We know that a giant asteroid—12 kilometers (7.5 miles) wide—walloped Earth 66 million years ago because we've found a chemical element called iridium. It's one of the rarest elements in the Earth's crust, but for some reason we have a thin, powdery layer of iridium deep down in our rock. Not only in China, Canada, or Australia, either. You'll find it all around the planet.

The only way this much iridium could be so evenly distributed around the world is if something very large and full of iridium smashed into our planet millions of years ago. That much energy would have created absolute chaos—darkening skies with ash, lowering the temperature, and killing plants and the dinosaurs that ate them. Eventually the meat-eating dinosaurs died, too. Only the small animals that didn't need much to eat survived.

Today you'll find the asteroid's impact point far below the ocean's surface in the Yucatán Peninsula of Mexico.

What would the world be like if dinosaurs were still alive?

Very, very different. Probably. Maybe. The fact is, nobody knows for sure how life would be different if ancient dinosaurs roamed the planet today.

Some experts believe mammals would still be really small and quick to avoid being eaten. Maybe humans never would have evolved at all! Or, if we did somehow exist side by side with dinos, it's likely we wouldn't have the technology we enjoy today. Rather than taking time to think up new inventions, we'd be spending it all running for our lives!

It's also possible that dinosaurs would look completely different now. Remember, they would have had 66 million more years to evolve and adapt to their surroundings. So who knows? Maybe their brains would have gotten bigger and smarter. In this parallel universe, young dinos could be going to school. A, B, C, D, EAT YOU UP!

Can we make dinosaurs from dino DNA?

It's never going to happen. The oldest DNA ever found is only about 700,000 years old. While that might sound ancient, dinosaurs died out roughly 66 million years ago. No dinosaur DNA survives, and it's highly unlikely we'll ever find any. (For more about DNA, read "Why is everybody different?" on page 42.) But even if we did have it, a baby dino would be used to living in a very different environment than what exists today on Earth. The balance of oxygen versus carbon dioxide has changed. So has the available food. The newborn dinosaur would likely die.

We do, however, have woolly mammoth DNA, and some scientists are looking into whether these giant beasts could be brought back to life using elephants as mothers. Possible? Yes. But just because we can clone a long-extinct animal, should we?

What do you think?

How did the Ice Age start?

Which one do you mean? There have been many major ice ages in Earth's history, going back at least 2.6 billion years.

The Earth spins on its own axis and orbits around the Sun. But like a spinning toy top, it eventually starts to wobble a bit. That wobble (called precession) exposes different parts of Earth's land to more or less sunlight and changes how much heat gets absorbed. Couple that effect with changes in greenhouse gases and say hello to your next ice age.

Because the planet is always slowly wobbling, we see a repeating pattern of long ice ages and shorter warm periods. Warm periods tend to last between 10,000 and 20,000 years—we're living in one right now. So when did the last ice age end? About 12,000 years ago.

While we might be ripe for another big one, humans have also been adding greenhouse gases to our atmosphere at a level that hasn't been seen on Earth for millions of years. Nobody is quite sure how climate change will impact our next ice age, or if another one will happen at all.

Snowball Earth

Some researchers believe that 650 million years ago, Earth was almost entirely covered in ice, from the North and South Poles to the tropics. There were only a few places on the entire planet where life could exist. Brrrr!

What is time?

Tough question. Some of the greatest minds of science still argue over what makes time tick. But most agree that time measures a sequence of events from past to future.

For centuries, people tracked time by looking around them. For instance, day turns into night. There's only one problem with these natural time-telling methods: they weren't precise. Sure, you could tell someone you wanted to meet them during the full Moon, but you might be waiting all night for them to show up! There had to be a better way.

Enter the clock. Seconds, minutes, and hours are really just convenient ways to divide time. Humans made them up! But now that we can tell time with accuracy, we communicate more easily with other people and make plans conveniently. Measuring time this way has its drawbacks, though. Who hasn't felt stressed trying to get to school on time?

Albert Einstein had thoughts about time, too. After years of deep thinking and studying the work of previous scientists, he made a connection between space and time: you can't experience one without the other. Let's say you want to hang out with a friend after school. You need to pick a place to meet, not just the time. Even if you run into each other in the hall, you're still meeting at a time and a place.

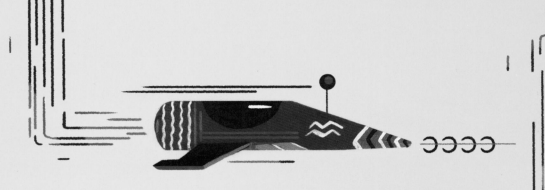

Is time travel possible?

Of course! We're always traveling in time. But as far as anyone can tell, we only go in one direction: forward. Yet while there's no way to reverse time, we can speed it up or slow it down. The secret? Travel away from Earth and/or move very fast!

Scientists have discovered that time speeds up when we move away from massive objects with a lot of gravity—our planet, for example. We see this in satellites far above Earth's surface. Clocks on those satellites tick faster up there than they do on the ground, where there's more gravity.

But we also know that time slows down as objects approach the speed of light. So if you were to launch yourself in a rocket and travel near the speed of light for 10 years on your clock, you might come back only a decade older—but 1,000 years will have passed on Earth!

An Accurate Clock? Great Timing!

An atomic clock keeps track of the internet's time. It's so accurate it will not lose or gain a second in 20 million years.

What hasn't been invented?

Who knows! An ice-cream cone with a big lip around the edge to catch the drippy parts? Sure! (Perfect for keeping away parents who insist on slurping the melting bits around the edge of their kids' cones—yuck.) A drone that follows you around and carries your backpack to school? Why not? An alarm clock that tickles you awake? Umm . . .

There are so many amazing inventions just waiting to be dreamed up. So, what would you invent? And, more important, what questions would you ask to get started today?

Conclusion

Cars, trains, and the world's fastest rockets.

The light beside your bed and the phone in your mom's hand.

Medicine that cures deadly diseases.

Even that cup of instant noodles you slurped up at lunch.

Each one of these creations exists today because people throughout history asked questions that led to scientific discoveries. Then inventors used those discoveries to make useful products and devices that would change the world.

Think Einstein could have dreamed that his questions about space, time, and gravity would eventually give computer programmers the scientific foundation they needed to make today's map software work properly? No way. But those questions did, even if it took many decades.

Science has the power to cure diseases, feed every person on the planet, build better homes, and power cars using nothing but the Sun's energy.

Want to learn more and spark new ideas and dreams of your own? That's what thousands of science centers around the world are all about. Maybe you have a science center close to where you live. You should visit! There's no better place to examine the wonders of the world above, below, and beyond the reaches of space.

So explore! Investigate! Visit a science center or science and technology museum! And don't forget to keep asking questions. You never know where they'll lead.

Acknowledgments

When I was a kid, I knew I wanted to do two things when I grew up:

1. Work at the Ontario Science Centre in Toronto, Ontario, my favorite place, ever.

2. Write books for kids.

With *Why Don't Cars Run on Apple Juice?*, I got to do both! (Even if that meant I simply got to wear a swanky Ontario Science Centre pass and feel like an employee for a couple of days.) A big thank you goes out to all the Science Centre staff, Rocio, Rachel, Walter, Julie, Oriana, Zoe, Jen, Catherine, Teressa, Russell, Martin, and Mary Jane. You provided your time, expertise, and loads of patience (not to mention a few props). Many thanks to Nicole Cavalluzzo for keeping the interviews on track, and Kevin von Appen for encouragement, guidance, and support. At Annick Press, much-deserved praise must go to Claire Caldwell, an author's dream editor who somehow balances being easygoing and hyper organized while still offering editing skills galore. A big shout-out to Kaela Cadieux, Paul Covello, Suharu Ogawa, Linda Pruessen, and DoEun Kwon. And of course Rick Wilks, who reached out and asked in the first place. Finally, to all the kids who provided questions for this book. (Yep, even the ones about poo.) This book is for you. It's a scientific fact!

—Kira Vermond

A remarkable team from the Ontario Science Centre pulled together to think about, talk about, laugh about, and answer these wonderful questions in a way that satisfies while sparking curiosity for more.

Catherine Birnie; Teressa Black; Nicole Cavaluzzo; Mary Jane Conboy, PhD; Martin Fischer; Zoe Fitzgerald; Karen Hager; Julie Jones; Jennifer O'Leary, PhD; Rocio Navarro; Enza Pacheco; Catherine Paisley; Anna Relyea; Lorrie Ann Smith; Walter Stoddard; Oriana Vella-Zarb; Kevin von Appen; Rachel Ward-Maxwell, PhD; Russell Zeid—thanks!

And a special thanks goes to Chris Caira, Lorraine Sit, and the rest of the Maker Bean Cafe staff at the Ontario Science Centre, who have gathered more than a thousand questions (and counting!) from visiting kids.

—Maurice Bitran, PhD
CEO, Ontario Science Centre

Huge thanks to the kids whose fascinating, thoughtful, creative, and wacky science questions made this book possible:

Anvj, Jordyn, Jacob, Sergio, Abbi, Rivka, Gloria, Atha, Rachella, Asher, Sylvia, Ryan, Ryan, Harrison, Kieran, Bella, Hyunchan, Stella, Elijah, Isaac, Amy, Lea, Samuel, Maya, Maya, Charlotte, Aubrey, Sara, Enoch, Ethan, Jennifer, Adam, Logan, Maggie, JJ, Rohan, Ayron, Vincent, Carter, Kashmir, Isha, Louise, Winston, Zachery, Hubert, Dani, Kaite, James, Grace, Reuel

Further Reading

Ayer, Paula, Antonia Banyard, and Belle Wuthrich. *Eat Up! An Infographic Exploration of Food*. Toronto: Annick Press, 2017

Carson, Mary Kay. Beyond the Solar System: *Exploring Galaxies, Black Holes, Alien Planets, and More*. Chicago: Chicago Review Press, 2013

Eamer, Claire, and Bambi Edlund. *What a Waste! Where Does Garbage Go?* Toronto: Annick Press, 2017

Hadfield, Chris. *You Are Here: Around the World in 92 minutes*. Toronto: Random House Canada, 2014

Jackson, Donna, and Ted Stearn. *What's So Funny? Making Sense of Humor*. New York: Viking, 2011

Select Sources

Secondary sources consulted by Kira Vermond.

CHAPTER 1: WHIPPING UP A BATCH OF PLANET EARTH

Why is ocean water salty?

NOAA, "Why is the ocean salty?," National Ocean Service website,
https://oceanservice.noaa.gov/facts/whysalty.html

NOAA, "Why is the ocean salty, but rivers flowing into it are not?," National Ocean Service website,
https://oceanservice.noaa.gov/facts/riversnotsalty.html

Why is some water turquoise and some water brown?

Lauren Phillips, "Why the Caribbean Sea Is So Blue," Coastal Living,
https://www.coastalliving.com/travel/other-coasts/why-is-caribbean-blue

NASA, "Ocean Color," NASA Science website, August 20, 2007,
https://science.nasa.gov/earth-science/oceanography/living-ocean/ocean-color

If metal sinks, how do boats float?

"Why can boats made of steel float on water when a bar of steel sinks?," How Stuff Works, April 1, 2000,
https://science.howstuffworks.com/science-vs-myth/everyday-myths/question254.htm

"Q & A: Why do ships float? Why don't they sink?," Ask the Van, University of Illinois at Urbana-Champaign Physics Department,
last updated March 5, 2011, https://van.physics.illinois.edu/qa/listing.php?id=2174

How does gravity keep us down?

NASA, "What is gravity?," NASA Space Place, last updated May 4, 2017, https://spaceplace.nasa.gov/what-is-gravity/en/

Julia Layton, "How does gravity work?," How Stuff Works, April 1, 2000,
https://science.howstuffworks.com/environmental/earth/geophysics/question232.htm

Where does wind come from?

Chris Weiss, "Where does wind come from?," *Scientific American* website, July 18, 2005,
https://www.scientificamerican.com/article/where-does-wind-come-from/

National Center for Families Learning, "Where Does Wind Come From?," Wonderopolis,
https://wonderopolis.org/wonder/where-does-wind-come-from

What came first, the tree or the seed?

David Biello, "How the First Plant Came to Be," *Scientific American* website, February 16, 2012,
https://www.scientificamerican.com/article/how-first-plant-evolved/

Brigitte Meyer-Berthaud, Stephen E. Scheckler, and Jobst Wendt, "*Archaeopteris* is the earliest known modern tree," Nature 398, 700–701,
April 22, 2009, https://www.nature.com/articles/19516

Ker Than, "World's First Tree Reconstructed," Live Science, April 18, 2007,
https://www.livescience.com/1439-world-tree-reconstructed.html

How do trees know about seasons?

Carl E. Palm Jr., "Why leaves change color . . . as featured on weather.com," SUNY College of Environmental Science and Forestry website,
https://www.esf.edu/pubprog/brochure/leaves/leaves.htm

Is there enough food in the world?

Barrett Colombo, Peder Engstrom, Deepak Ray, Andrew Urevig, and Paul West, "Is There Enough Food for the Future?," *Environment Reports*: Food Matters, http://www.environmentreports.com/enough-food-for-the-future/

Oliver Milman, "Americans waste 150,000 tons of food each day — equal to a pound per person," *The Guardian* website, April 18, 2018, https://www.theguardian.com/environment/2018/apr/18/americans-waste-food-fruit-vegetables-study

Why don't cars run on apple juice?

"Learning About Calories," reviewed by Mary L. Gavin, MD, June 2018, KidsHealth from Nemours, https://kidshealth.org/en/kids/calorie.html

CHAPTER 2: CREEPING, CRAWLING LIVING THINGS

Why do worms come out when it rains?

Rhonda Sherman, "How do earthworms eat and poop — and other surprising facts," *The Washington Post* website, April 21, 2017, https://www.washingtonpost.com/national/health-science/how-do-night-crawlers-eat-and-poop--and-other-surprising-facts/2017/04/21/ebe2a8ac-13ee-11e7-ada0-1489b735b3a3_story.html?noredirect=on&utm_term=.39849a86a403

Why do we have different faces but ants do not?

"Ant Facts for Kids," PestWorld for Kids website, https://pestworldforkids.org/pest-guide/ants/

Why can't you live with a wolf?

Elizabeth Pennisi, "What makes dogs so friendly? Study finds genetic link to super-outgoing people," *Science* website, July 19, 2017, http://www.sciencemag.org/news/2017/07/what-makes-dogs-so-friendly-study-finds-genetic-link-super-outgoing-people

If a dog says "woof!" will other dogs understand?

"Why Do Dogs Wag Their Tails?," Animal Planet website, http://www.animalplanet.com/pets/why-do-dogs-wag-their-tails/

How many unfound species are there in the world?

National Center for Families Learning, "How Many Animals Are There in the World?," Wonderopolis, https://wonderopolis.org/wonder/how-many-animals-are-there-in-the-world

Roskov Y., L. Abucay, T. Orrell, D. Nicolson, N. Bailly, P.M. Kirk, T. Bourgoin, R.E. DeWalt, W. Decock, A. De Wever, E. van Nieukerken, J. Zarucchi, L. Peney, eds. Species 2000 & ITIS Catalogue of Life, 2018 Annual Checklist, www.catalogueoflife.org/annual-checklist/2018. *Species 2000: Naturalis*, Leiden, the Netherlands. ISSN 2405-884X.

"How many species are we losing?," World Wildlife Fund website, http://wwf.panda.org/our_work/biodiversity/biodiversity/

Eye-catching shark!

Kimberly Hickok, "This Big-Eyed, Deep-Sea Shark Looks Like an Anime Character," Live Science, July 17, 2018, https://www.livescience.com/63086-new-genies-dogfish-shark.html

CHAPTER 3: HUMAN BODIES FROM THE INSIDE OUT

Why do my toots smell?

"The Science of Farting," Kidzworld, December 27, 2006, https://www.kidzworld.com/article/473-the-science-of-farting

Why can't humans breathe underwater?

"If water is made up of hydrogen and oxygen, why can't we breathe underwater?," How Stuff Works, May 23, 2000, https://science.howstuffworks.com/question386.htm

Why is everybody different?

Hannah Ashworth, "How long is your DNA?," *Science Focus* website, https://www.sciencefocus.com/the-human-body/how-long-is-your-dna/

"What is DNA?," BBC Bitesize, https://www.bbc.com/bitesize/articles/zvwbcj6

C. Claiborne Ray, "Twins and Fingerprints," *The New York Times* website, October 5, 2009, https://www.nytimes.com/2009/10/06/science/06qna.html

How do people think without language?

Arika Okrent, "Is It Possible To Think Without Language?," Mental Floss, May 23 , 2013,
http://mentalfloss.com/article/50684/it-possible-think-without-language

Why do people find things funny? Why is everyone so funny?

Alex Borgella, "Science deconstructs humor: What makes some things funny?," The Conversation, November 1, 2016,
http://theconversation.com/science-deconstructs-humor-what-makes-some-things-funny-64414

Why do people need to sleep?

"Why Do We Sleep, Anyway?," Healthy Sleep website, Division of Sleep Medicine at Harvard Medical School,
http://healthysleep.med.harvard.edu/healthy/matters/benefits-of-sleep/why-do-we-sleep

Why do we die?

"Your Heart & Circulatory System," reviewed by Steven Dowshen, MD, May 2018, KidsHealth from Nemours,
https://kidshealth.org/en/kids/heart.html

Corey Binns, "Why Do We Die?," Live Science, February 6, 2013, https://www.livescience.com/32477-why-do-we-die.html

CHAPTER 4: STARS, MOONS, PLANETS, AND OUTER SPACE

Are there creatures on other planets?

Nola Taylor Redd, "Life on Mars: Exploration & Evidence," Space.com, December 15, 2017,
https://www.space.com/17135-life-on-mars.html

Stuart Gary, "What is the Goldilocks Zone and why does it matter in the search for ET?," ABC News website, February 21, 2016,
https://www.abc.net.au/news/science/2016-02-22/goldilocks-zones-habitable-zone-astrobiology-exoplanets/6907836

What happens inside a black hole?

Heather R. Smith, "What Is a Black Hole?," NASA Knows! (Grades K–4) series, August 21, 2018,
https://www.nasa.gov/audience/forstudents/k-4/stories/nasa-knows/what-is-a-black-hole-k4.html

Heather R. Smith, "What Is a Black Hole?," NASA Knows! (Grades 5–8) series, last updated August 7, 2017,
https://www.nasa.gov/audience/forstudents/5-8/features/nasa-knows/what-is-a-black-hole-58.html

Will another asteroid hit Earth?

NASA, "Asteroid Fast Facts," NASA website, last updated August 7, 2017,
https://www.nasa.gov/mission_pages/asteroids/overview/fastfacts.html

Can sound move in space?

David Nield, "Sound Can Travel Through Space After All — But We Can't Hear It," ScienceAlert, October 30, 2015,
https://www.sciencealert.com/sound-can-travel-through-space-after-all-but-we-can-t-hear-it

What causes a solar eclipse?

Brandi Bernoskie and Heather Deiss, "What Is an Eclipse?," NASA Knows! (Grades 5–8) series, May 3, 2017,
https://www.nasa.gov/audience/forstudents/5-8/features/nasa-knows/what-is-an-eclipse-58

Dave Kornreich, "Why do we not have eclipses every month? (Beginner)," Ask an Astronomer, Astronomy Department at Cornell University,
http://curious.astro.cornell.edu/people-and-astronomy/127-observational-astronomy/lunar-and-solar-eclipses/general-questions/775-why-do-we-not-have-eclipses-every-month-beginner

"Lunar Eclipses and Solar Eclipses," last updated June 20, 2017, NASA Space Place, https://spaceplace.nasa.gov/eclipses/en/

If the universe is expanding, then what's outside the universe?

Dave Rothstein, "What is the universe expanding into? (Intermediate)," Ask an Astronomer, Astronomy Department at Cornell University, last updated June 27, 2015, http://curious.astro.cornell.edu/people-and-astronomy/104-the-universe/cosmology-and-the-big-bang/expansion-of-the-universe/623-what-is-the-universe-expanding-into-intermediate

Jolene Creighton, "What Lies Beyond the Edge of the Observable Universe?," Futurism website, February 23, 2014, https://futurism.com/what-lies-beyond-the-edge-of-the-observable-universe/

Fraser Cain, "What is the Universe Expanding Into?," Universe Today website, November 28, 2013, https://www.universetoday.com/1455/podcast-what-is-the-universe-expanding-into/

Fraser Cain, "Is the Universe Finite or Infinite?," Universe Today website, March 26, 2015, https://www.universetoday.com/119553/is-the-universe-finite-or-infinite/

CHAPTER 5: BIG IDEAS PAST, PRESENT, AND FUTURE

How did we discover the Big Bang?

"How do we know the Big Bang happened?," BBC Science, January 8, 2013, http://www.bbc.co.uk/science/0/20932483

An amazing Big Bang accident!

Alaina G. Levine, "Arno Penzias and Robert Wilson. Bell Labs, Holmdel, NJ. The Large Horn Antenna and the Discovery of Cosmic Microwave Background Radiation," American Physical Society website, https://www.aps.org/programs/outreach/history/historicsites/penziaswilson.cfm

Mike Wall, "Cosmic Anniversary: 'Big Bang Echo' Discovered 50 Years Ago Today," Space.com, May 20, 2014, https://www.space.com/25945-cosmic-microwave-background-discovery-50th-anniversary.html

Big Bang blunder

"How Long Did the Big Bang Last?," yeWonder, June 2, 2015, http://yewonder.com/2027-how-long-did-the-big-bang-last.html

Patagotitan mayorum: the BIGGEST dino of all?

Ed Yong, "Meet Patagotitan, the Biggest Dinosaur Ever Found," *The Atlantic* website, August 8, 2017, https://www.theatlantic.com/science/archive/2017/08/is-this-really-the-biggest-dinosaur-ever-discovered/536187/

How do we really know a meteor killed the dinosaurs?

Michelle Z. Donahue, "Dino-Killing Asteroid Hit Just the Right Spot to Trigger Extinction," *National Geographic* website, November 9, 2017, https://news.nationalgeographic.com/2017/11/dinosaurs-extinction-asteroid-chicxulub-soot-earth-science/

What is time?

Adam Mann, "How the U.S. Built the World's Most Ridiculously Accurate Atomic Clock," *Wired* website, April 4, 2014, https://www.wired.com/2014/04/nist-atomic-clock/

"The History of Timekeeping," Kids Geography, Kids Know It Network, https://kidsgeo.com/geography-for-kids/history-of-timekeeping/ (site discontinued)

Note to readers: The statistics in this book are drawn from the latest information available at press time. In cases where numbers may vary, averages have been used. Unless otherwise noted, all online sources were last consulted between November 2018 and March 2019.

Index